GRATITUDE

with

Attitude

For Boys
10-15 YRS

Name - - - - - - - - - - - - -

Starting Date

Day   Month   Year

The Life Graduate Publishing Group

Stronger Friendships

Kindness and Appreciation

The benefits of
GRATITUDE
(What you are thankful for)

Better Health

Increased Energy

Greater Sleep Quality

The Importance of Gratitude

Congratulations on starting your very own Gratitude Journal. By completing your journal each day, it will help you to appreciate all of the great things around you!

This journal has been created especially for boys in a clear, easy and interactive one page format to make it both enjoyable and simple for you to write down how you feel, the things you enjoyed during the day and also includes spaces for sketches or photos if you choose.

The journal asks you to write down 2 or 3 things each day that you're grateful for. These may be things that have happened during the day, during the week or something happening in your life right now? To help you, it could be things that you do with family and friends like vacations, the accomplishments you have earned at school, sports events or activities, new friendships you have formed or anything else that you are grateful for.

Just sparing a few minutes each day to think about the things in life that matter to you will boost your confidence, energy levels and you will take new leaps and bounds every day.

Gratitude and mindfulness activities like journaling are so important, and we all need to think about what we are grateful for every day.

Wishing you all the very best!

Romney

Romney Nelson - Teacher & Multiple Best Selling Author
Founder - The Life Graduate Publishing Group
www.thelifegraduate.com

How to use your journal

Step 1.

Complete your journal in a location that you can be clear of distractions.

Step 2.

Follow the prompts on each page. Start by writing down the day and date and then move onto the first question.

Step 3.

Write down exactly how you feel. Being honest with ourselves is an important start on our gratitude journey.

Step 4.

Once completed, place in a safe place and in a location that will remind you to complete the journal tomorrow. To help, it is sometimes good to set a daily alarm for the same time each day.

GRATTITUDE
with
Attitude

CIRCLE THE DAY

DAY: MON TUES WED THU FRI SAT SUN

DATE

___ / ___ / ___

01 GRATITUDE

Today I am *Grateful* for:

_____

_____

02 THANKFULNESS

This person helped me out today:

03 KNOWLEDGE & LEARNING

Today I learned:

_____

_____

DAY: MON TUES WED THU FRI SAT SUN

DATE

___ / ___ / ___

01 GRATITUDE

Today I am *Grateful* for:

_____

_____

02 MY ENERGY

My **Energy Level** today:

Circle how you feel

I feel this way because:

_____

_____

GRATTITUDE with Attitude

CIRCLE THE DAY

DAY: MON TUES WED THU FRI SAT SUN

DATE __/__/__

01 GRATITUDE
Today I am *Grateful* for:

_____

_____

02 THANKFULNESS
This person helped me out today:

03 KNOWLEDGE & LEARNING
Today I learned:

_____

DAY: MON TUES WED THU FRI SAT SUN

DATE __/__/__

01 GRATITUDE
Today I am *Grateful* for:

_____

_____

02 CONNECTIVITY
How 'connected' did you feel to others today?

Tick a circle ➤

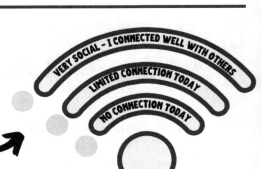

VERY SOCIAL – I CONNECTED WELL WITH OTHERS

LIMITED CONNECTION TODAY

NO CONNECTION TODAY

GRATTITUDE
with
Attitude

DAY: MON TUES WED THU FRI SAT SUN

01 GRATITUDE

Today I am *Grateful* for:

DATE

___ / ___ / ___

_____

_____

02 THANKFULNESS

This person helped me out today:

03 KNOWLEDGE & LEARNING

Today I learned:

_____

DAY: MON TUES WED THU FRI SAT SUN

01 GRATITUDE

Today I am *Grateful* for:

DATE

___ / ___ / ___

_____

_____

02 ACT OF KINDNESS

I helped this person out today:_____

I helped them by...

_____

GRATTITUDE
with
Attitude

DAY: MON TUES WED THU FRI SAT SUN

DATE

___ / ___ / ___

01 GRATITUDE
Today I am *Grateful* for:

_____

_____

02 THANKFULNESS
This person helped me out today:

03 KNOWLEDGE & LEARNING
Today I learned:

_____

DAY: MON TUES WED THU FRI SAT SUN

DATE

___ / ___ / ___

01 GRATITUDE
Today I am *Grateful* for:

_____

02 THIS PUT A SMILE ON MY FACE

Today I smiled when:

_____

_____

GRATTITUDE
with
Attitude

DAY: MON TUES WED THU FRI SAT SUN

DATE
___/___/___

01 GRATITUDE
Today I am *Grateful* for:

_____

_____

02 THANKFULNESS
This person helped me out today:

03 KNOWLEDGE & LEARNING
Today I learned:

_____

DAY: MON TUES WED THU FRI SAT SUN

DATE
___/___/___

01 GRATITUDE
Today I am *Grateful* for:

_____

_____

02 THIS PUT A SMILE ON MY FACE
Today I smiled when:

_____

_____

GRATTITUDE
with
Attitude

DAY: MON TUES WED THU FRI SAT SUN

DATE

___/___/___

01 GRATITUDE
Today I am *Grateful* for:

_____

_____

02 THANKFULNESS
This person helped me out today:

03 KNOWLEDGE & LEARNING
Today I learned:

_____

DAY: MON TUES WED THU FRI SAT SUN

DATE

___/___/___

01 GRATITUDE
Today I am *Grateful* for:

_____

_____

02 MY ENERGY
My **Energy Level** today:

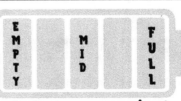

Circle how you feel

I feel this way because:

_____

_____

GRATTITUDE
with
Attitude

DAY: **MON TUES WED THU FRI SAT SUN**

DATE
___/___/___

01 GRATITUDE
Today I am *Grateful* for:

_____

_____

02 THANKFULNESS
This person helped me out today:

03 KNOWLEDGE & LEARNING
Today I learned:

_____

DAY: **MON TUES WED THU FRI SAT SUN**

DATE
___/___/___

01 GRATITUDE
Today I am *Grateful* for:

_____

_____

02 CONNECTIVITY
How 'connected' did you feel to others today?

Tick a circle ➜

VERY SOCIAL - I CONNECTED WELL WITH OTHERS

LIMITED CONNECTION TODAY

NO CONNECTION TODAY

GRATITUDE
with
Attitude

CIRCLE THE DAY

DAY: MON TUES WED THU FRI SAT SUN

DATE
___/___/___

01 GRATITUDE
Today I am *Grateful* for:

_____

_____

02 THANKFULNESS
This person helped me out today:

03 KNOWLEDGE & LEARNING
Today I learned:

_____

DAY: MON TUES WED THU FRI SAT SUN

DATE
___/___/___

01 GRATITUDE
Today I am *Grateful* for:

_____

_____

02 ACT OF KINDNESS
I helped this person out today:_____

I helped them by...

_____

GRATTITUDE
with
Attitude

CIRCLE THE DAY

DAY: MON TUES WED THU FRI SAT SUN

DATE
_/_/_

01 GRATITUDE
Today I am *Grateful* for:

_____

_____

02 THANKFULNESS
This person helped me out today:

03 KNOWLEDGE & LEARNING
Today I learned:

_____

DAY: MON TUES WED THU FRI SAT SUN

DATE
_/_/_

01 GRATITUDE
Today I am *Grateful* for:

_____

_____

02 THIS PUT A SMILE ON MY FACE

Today I smiled when:

_____

_____

GRATTITUDE
with
Attitude

CIRCLE THE DAY

DAY: MON TUES WED THU FRI SAT SUN

DATE
_ / _ / _

01 GRATITUDE
Today I am *Grateful* for:

_____

_____

02 THANKFULNESS
This person helped me out today:

03 KNOWLEDGE & LEARNING
Today I learned:

_____

DAY: MON TUES WED THU FRI SAT SUN

DATE
_ / _ / _

01 GRATITUDE
Today I am *Grateful* for:

_____

_____

02 THIS PUT A SMILE ON MY FACE

Today I smiled when:

_____

_____

GRATTITUDE
with
Attitude

DAY: **MON TUES WED THU FRI SAT SUN**

DATE
___/___/___

01 GRATITUDE
Today I am *Grateful* for:

_____

_____

02 THANKFULNESS
This person helped me out today:

03 KNOWLEDGE & LEARNING
Today I learned:

_____

DAY: **MON TUES WED THU FRI SAT SUN**

DATE
___/___/___

01 GRATITUDE
Today I am *Grateful* for:

_____

_____

02 MY ENERGY

My **Energy Level** today:

Circle how you feel

I feel this way because:

_____

_____

GRATTITUDE
with
Attitude

DAY: MON TUES WED THU FRI SAT SUN

DATE

/ /

01 GRATITUDE

Today I am *Grateful* for:

_____

_____

02 THANKFULNESS

This person helped me out today:

03 KNOWLEDGE & LEARNING

Today I learned:

_____

DAY: MON TUES WED THU FRI SAT SUN

DATE

/ /

01 GRATITUDE

Today I am *Grateful* for:

_____

_____

02 CONNECTIVITY

How 'connected' did you feel to others today?

Tick a circle

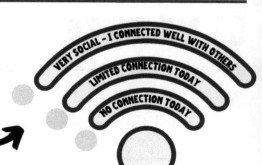

VERY SOCIAL – I CONNECTED WELL WITH OTHERS

LIMITED CONNECTION TODAY

NO CONNECTION TODAY

GRATTITUDE
with
Attitude

DAY: MON TUES WED THU FRI SAT SUN

DATE

__ / __ / __

01 GRATITUDE

Today I am *Grateful* for:

_____

_____

02 THANKFULNESS

This person helped me out today:

03 KNOWLEDGE & LEARNING

Today I learned:

_____

DAY: MON TUES WED THU FRI SAT SUN

DATE

__ / __ / __

01 GRATITUDE

Today I am *Grateful* for:

_____

_____

02 ACT OF KINDNESS

I helped this person out today:_____

I helped them by...

_____

GRATTITUDE
with
Attitude

DAY: MON TUES WED THU FRI SAT SUN

DATE
___/___/___

01 GRATITUDE
Today I am *Grateful* for:

_____

_____

02 THANKFULNESS
This person helped me out today:

03 KNOWLEDGE & LEARNING
Today I learned:

_____

DAY: MON TUES WED THU FRI SAT SUN

DATE
___/___/___

01 GRATITUDE
Today I am *Grateful* for:

_____

_____

02 THIS PUT A SMILE ON MY FACE
Today I smiled when:

_____

_____

GRATTITUDE
with
Attitude

DAY: MON TUES WED THU FRI SAT SUN

01 GRATITUDE
Today I am *Grateful* for:

_____

_____

02 THANKFULNESS
This person helped me out today:

03 KNOWLEDGE & LEARNING
Today I learned:

_____

DAY: MON TUES WED THU FRI SAT SUN

01 GRATITUDE
Today I am *Grateful* for:

_____

_____

02 THIS PUT A SMILE ON MY FACE
Today I smiled when:

_____

_____

30

GRATTITUDE
with
Attitude

CONGRATULATIONS! YOU ARE UP TO DAY 30

IT'S TIME FOR YOU TO LOOK BACK OVER YOUR GRATITUDE JOURNAL AND ANSWER THE FOLLOWING QUESTIONS.

01 MOMENTS

What were your favorite 3 things you did over the past 30 days?

1. _____

2. _____

3. _____

02 Be Creative!

Sketch a picture, stick in a photo or include here something that was special for you over the past 30 days.

MEMENTO

GRATITUDE WITH ATTITUDE
JOURNAL

Print something up, include a certificate, an award from school or even find something from outside that you can include here. It will be great to reflect back on this after you have completed your journal.

GRATTITUDE
with
Attitude

DAY: **MON TUES WED THU FRI SAT SUN**

DATE
___/___/___

01 GRATITUDE
Today I am *Grateful* for:

_____

_____

02 THANKFULNESS
This person helped me out today:

03 KNOWLEDGE & LEARNING
Today I learned:

_____

DAY: **MON TUES WED THU FRI SAT SUN**

DATE
___/___/___

01 GRATITUDE
Today I am *Grateful* for:

_____

_____

02 MY ENERGY
My **Energy Level** today:

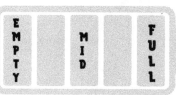

Circle how you feel

I feel this way because:

_____

_____

GRATTITUDE
with
Attitude

CIRCLE THE DAY

DAY: MON TUES WED THU FRI SAT SUN

DATE

___ / ___ / ___

01 GRATITUDE

Today I am *Grateful* for:

_____

_____

02 THANKFULNESS

This person helped me out today:

03 KNOWLEDGE & LEARNING

Today I learned:

_____

DAY: MON TUES WED THU FRI SAT SUN

DATE

___ / ___ / ___

01 GRATITUDE

Today I am *Grateful* for:

_____

_____

02 CONNECTIVITY

How 'connected' did you feel to others today?

Tick a circle

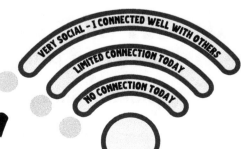

VERY SOCIAL – I CONNECTED WELL WITH OTHERS

LIMITED CONNECTION TODAY

NO CONNECTION TODAY

GRATTITUDE
with
Attitude

DAY: MON TUES WED THU FRI SAT SUN

DATE

01 GRATITUDE

Today I am *Grateful* for:

_____

_____

02 THANKFULNESS

This person helped me out today:

03 KNOWLEDGE & LEARNING

Today I learned:

_____

DAY: MON TUES WED THU FRI SAT SUN

DATE

01 GRATITUDE

Today I am *Grateful* for:

_____

_____

02 ACT OF KINDNESS

I helped this person out today: _____

I helped them by...

_____

GRATTITUDE
with
Attitude

CIRCLE THE DAY

DAY: MON TUES WED THU FRI SAT SUN

DATE

___/___/___

01 GRATITUDE
Today I am *Grateful* for:

_____

_____

02 THANKFULNESS
This person helped me out today:

03 KNOWLEDGE & LEARNING
Today I learned:

_____

DAY: MON TUES WED THU FRI SAT SUN

DATE

___/___/___

01 GRATITUDE
Today I am *Grateful* for:

_____

_____

02 THIS PUT A SMILE ON MY FACE

Today I smiled when:

_____

_____

GRATTITUDE
with
Attitude

DAY: MON TUES WED THU FRI SAT SUN

01 GRATITUDE

Today I am *Grateful* for:

DATE

___ / ___ / ___

_____

_____

02 THANKFULNESS

This person helped me out today:

03 KNOWLEDGE & LEARNING

Today I learned:

_____

DAY: MON TUES WED THU FRI SAT SUN

01 GRATITUDE

Today I am *Grateful* for:

DATE

___ / ___ / ___

_____

_____

02 THIS PUT A SMILE ON MY FACE

Today I smiled when:

_____

_____

GRATTITUDE
with
Attitude

CIRCLE THE DAY

DAY: MON TUES WED THU FRI SAT SUN

DATE
___/___/___

01 GRATITUDE
Today I am *Grateful* for:

_____

_____

02 THANKFULNESS
This person helped me out today:

03 KNOWLEDGE & LEARNING
Today I learned:

_____

DAY: MON TUES WED THU FRI SAT SUN

DATE
___/___/___

01 GRATITUDE
Today I am *Grateful* for:

_____

_____

02 MY ENERGY
My **Energy Level** today:

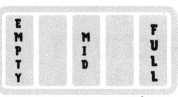

Circle how you feel

I feel this way because:

_____

_____

GRATITUDE with Attitude

CIRCLE THE DAY

DAY: MON TUES WED THU FRI SAT SUN

DATE
___/___/___

01 GRATITUDE
Today I am *Grateful* for:

_____

_____

02 THANKFULNESS
This person helped me out today:

03 KNOWLEDGE & LEARNING
Today I learned:

_____

DAY: MON TUES WED THU FRI SAT SUN

DATE
___/___/___

01 GRATITUDE
Today I am *Grateful* for:

_____

_____

02 CONNECTIVITY
How 'connected' did you feel to others today?

Tick a circle

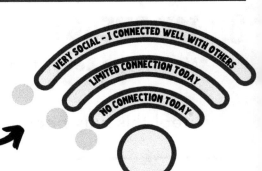

VERY SOCIAL – I CONNECTED WELL WITH OTHERS
LIMITED CONNECTION TODAY
NO CONNECTION TODAY

DAY: MON TUES WED THU FRI SAT SUN

DATE
___/___/___

01 GRATITUDE
Today I am *Grateful* for:

_____

_____

02 THANKFULNESS
This person helped me out today:

03 KNOWLEDGE & LEARNING
Today I learned:

_____

DAY: MON TUES WED THU FRI SAT SUN

DATE
___/___/___

01 GRATITUDE
Today I am *Grateful* for:

_____

_____

02 ACT OF KINDNESS

I helped this person out today: _____

I helped them by...

_____

GRATTITUDE
with
Attitude

DAY: MON TUES WED THU FRI SAT SUN

DATE

___/___/___

01 GRATITUDE

Today I am *Grateful* for:

_____

_____

02 THANKFULNESS

This person helped me out today:

03 KNOWLEDGE & LEARNING

Today I learned:

_____

DAY: MON TUES WED THU FRI SAT SUN

DATE

___/___/___

01 GRATITUDE

Today I am *Grateful* for:

_____

_____

02 THIS PUT A SMILE ON MY FACE

Today I smiled when:

_____

_____

GRATTITUDE
with
Attitude

DAY: MON TUES WED THU FRI SAT SUN

01 GRATITUDE

DATE
____ / ____ / ____

Today I am *Grateful* for:

_____

_____

02 THANKFULNESS

This person helped me out today:

03 KNOWLEDGE & LEARNING

Today I learned:

_____

DAY: MON TUES WED THU FRI SAT SUN

01 GRATITUDE

DATE
____ / ____ / ____

Today I am *Grateful* for:

_____

_____

02 THIS PUT A SMILE ON MY FACE

Today I smiled when:

_____

_____

GRATTITUDE
with
Attitude

DAY: MON TUES WED THU FRI SAT SUN

DATE

___ / ___ / ___

01 GRATITUDE

Today I am *Grateful* for:

_____

_____

02 THANKFULNESS

This person helped me out today:

03 KNOWLEDGE & LEARNING

Today I learned:

_____

DAY: MON TUES WED THU FRI SAT SUN

DATE

___ / ___ / ___

01 GRATITUDE

Today I am *Grateful* for:

_____

_____

02 MY ENERGY

My **Energy Level** today:

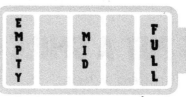

EMPTY | MID | FULL

Circle how you feel

I feel this way because:

_____

_____

GRATTITUDE
with
Attitude

CIRCLE THE DAY

DAY: **MON TUES WED THU FRI SAT SUN**

DATE

___ / ___ / ___

01 GRATITUDE

Today I am *Grateful* for:

_____

_____

02 THANKFULNESS

This person helped me out today:

03 KNOWLEDGE & LEARNING

Today I learned:

_____

DAY: **MON TUES WED THU FRI SAT SUN**

DATE

___ / ___ / ___

01 GRATITUDE

Today I am *Grateful* for:

_____

_____

02 CONNECTIVITY

How 'connected' did you feel to others today?

Tick a circle

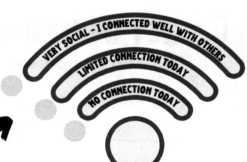

VERY SOCIAL - I CONNECTED WELL WITH OTHERS

LIMITED CONNECTION TODAY

NO CONNECTION TODAY

GRATTITUDE
with
Attitude

CIRCLE THE DAY

DAY: MON TUES WED THU FRI SAT SUN

DATE
__ / __ / __

01 GRATITUDE

Today I am *Grateful* for:

_____

_____

02 THANKFULNESS

This person helped me out today:

03 KNOWLEDGE & LEARNING

Today I learned:

_____

DAY: MON TUES WED THU FRI SAT SUN

DATE
__ / __ / __

01 GRATITUDE

Today I am *Grateful* for:

_____

_____

02 ACT OF KINDNESS

I helped this person out today: _____

I helped them by...

_____

GRATTITUDE
with
Attitude

DAY: MON TUES WED THU FRI SAT SUN

DATE
/ /

01 GRATITUDE
Today I am *Grateful* for:

_____

_____

02 THANKFULNESS
This person helped me out today:

03 KNOWLEDGE & LEARNING
Today I learned:

_____

DAY: MON TUES WED THU FRI SAT SUN

DATE
/ /

01 GRATITUDE
Today I am *Grateful* for:

_____

02 THIS PUT A SMILE ON MY FACE
Today I smiled when:

_____

_____

GRATTITUDE
with
Attitude

CIRCLE THE DAY

DAY: MON TUES WED THU FRI SAT SUN

DATE
___ / ___ / ___

01 GRATITUDE
Today I am *Grateful* for:

_____

_____

02 THANKFULNESS
This person helped me out today:

03 KNOWLEDGE & LEARNING
Today I learned:

_____

DAY: MON TUES WED THU FRI SAT SUN

DATE
___ / ___ / ___

01 GRATITUDE
Today I am *Grateful* for:

_____

_____

02 THIS PUT A SMILE ON MY FACE
Today I smiled when:

_____

_____

 **CIRCLE THE DAY**

GRATTITUDE
with
Attitude

DAY: MON TUES WED THU FRI SAT SUN

DATE
___/___/___

01 GRATITUDE

Today I am *Grateful* for:

_____

_____

02 THANKFULNESS

This person helped me out today:

03 KNOWLEDGE & LEARNING

Today I learned:

_____

DAY: MON TUES WED THU FRI SAT SUN

DATE
___/___/___

01 GRATITUDE

Today I am *Grateful* for:

_____

_____

02 MY ENERGY

My **Energy Level** today:

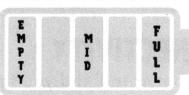

Circle how you feel

I feel this way because:

_____

_____

GRATTITUDE
with
Attitude

CIRCLE THE DAY

DAY: MON TUES WED THU FRI SAT SUN

DATE __ / __ / __

01 GRATITUDE
Today I am *Grateful* for:

_____

_____

02 THANKFULNESS
This person helped me out today:

03 KNOWLEDGE & LEARNING
Today I learned:

_____

DAY: MON TUES WED THU FRI SAT SUN

DATE __ / __ / __

01 GRATITUDE
Today I am *Grateful* for:

_____

_____

02 CONNECTIVITY
How 'connected' did you feel to others today?

Tick a circle ➤

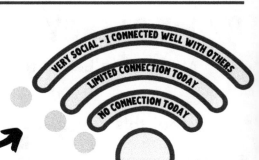

VERY SOCIAL – I CONNECTED WELL WITH OTHERS

LIMITED CONNECTION TODAY

NO CONNECTION TODAY

GRATTITUDE
with
Attitude

DAY: MON TUES WED THU FRI SAT SUN

DATE

___ / ___ / ___

01 GRATITUDE
Today I am *Grateful* for:

_____

_____

02 THANKFULNESS
This person helped me out today:

03 KNOWLEDGE & LEARNING
Today I learned:

_____

DAY: MON TUES WED THU FRI SAT SUN

DATE
___ / ___ / ___

01 GRATITUDE
Today I am *Grateful* for:

_____

_____

02 ACT OF KINDNESS
I helped this person out today: _____

I helped them by...

_____

GRATTITUDE
with
Attitude

DAY: MON TUES WED THU FRI SAT SUN

DATE

___ / ___ / ___

01 GRATITUDE

Today I am *Grateful* for:

_____

_____

02 THANKFULNESS

This person helped me out today:

03 KNOWLEDGE & LEARNING

Today I learned:

_____

DAY: MON TUES WED THU FRI SAT SUN

DATE

___ / ___ / ___

01 GRATITUDE

Today I am *Grateful* for:

_____

_____

02 THIS PUT A SMILE ON MY FACE

Today I smiled when:

_____

_____

GRATTITUDE
with
Attitude

01 GRATITUDE

DATE

___ / ___ / ___

Today I am *Grateful* for:

_____

_____

02 THANKFULNESS

This person helped me out today:

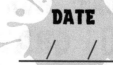

03 KNOWLEDGE & LEARNING

Today I learned:

_____

01 GRATITUDE

DATE

___ / ___ / ___

Today I am *Grateful* for:

_____

_____

02 THIS PUT A SMILE ON MY FACE

Today I smiled when:

_____

_____

 **CIRCLE THE DAY**

GRATTITUDE
with
Attitude

DAY: MON TUES WED THU FRI SAT SUN

DATE

___ / ___ / ___

01 GRATITUDE

Today I am *Grateful* for:

_____

_____

02 THANKFULNESS

This person helped me out today:

03 KNOWLEDGE & LEARNING

Today I learned:

_____

DAY: MON TUES WED THU FRI SAT SUN

DATE

___ / ___ / ___

01 GRATITUDE

Today I am *Grateful* for:

_____

_____

02 MY ENERGY

My **Energy Level** today:

Circle how you feel

I feel this way because:

_____

GRATTITUDE
with
Attitude

DAY: MON TUES WED THU FRI SAT SUN

01 GRATITUDE

Today I am *Grateful* for:

DATE
___/___/___

02 THANKFULNESS

This person helped me out today:

03 KNOWLEDGE & LEARNING

Today I learned:

DAY: MON TUES WED THU FRI SAT SUN

01 GRATITUDE

Today I am *Grateful* for:

DATE
___/___/___

02 CONNECTIVITY

How 'connected' did you feel to others today?

Tick a circle

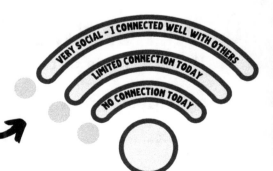

VERY SOCIAL – I CONNECTED WELL WITH OTHERS

LIMITED CONNECTION TODAY

NO CONNECTION TODAY

GRATTITUDE
with
Attitude

DAY: MON TUES WED THU FRI SAT SUN

DATE

___ / ___ / ___

01 GRATITUDE
Today I am *Grateful* for:

_____

_____

02 THANKFULNESS
This person helped me out today:

03 KNOWLEDGE & LEARNING
Today I learned:

_____

DAY: MON TUES WED THU FRI SAT SUN

DATE

___ / ___ / ___

01 GRATITUDE
Today I am *Grateful* for:

_____

_____

02 ACT OF KINDNESS
I helped this person out today:_____

I helped them by...

_____

GRATTITUDE
with
Attitude

DAY: MON TUES WED THU FRI SAT SUN

DATE

___ / ___ / ___

01 GRATITUDE
Today I am *Grateful* for:

_____

_____

02 THANKFULNESS
This person helped me out today:

03 KNOWLEDGE & LEARNING
Today I learned:

_____

DAY: MON TUES WED THU FRI SAT SUN

DATE

___ / ___ / ___

01 GRATITUDE
Today I am *Grateful* for:

_____

02 THIS PUT A SMILE ON MY FACE

Today I smiled when:

_____

_____

GRATTITUDE with Attitude

DAY: MON TUES WED THU FRI SAT SUN

DATE
___/___/___

01 GRATITUDE
Today I am *Grateful* for:

_____

_____

02 THANKFULNESS
This person helped me out today:

03 KNOWLEDGE & LEARNING
Today I learned:

_____

DAY: MON TUES WED THU FRI SAT SUN

DATE
___/___/___

01 GRATITUDE
Today I am *Grateful* for:

_____

_____

02 THIS PUT A SMILE ON MY FACE

Today I smiled when:

_____

_____

GRATTITUDE
with
Attitude

DAY: MON TUES WED THU FRI SAT SUN

DATE

___/___/___

01 GRATITUDE
Today I am *Grateful* for:

_____

_____

02 THANKFULNESS
This person helped me out today:

03 KNOWLEDGE & LEARNING
Today I learned:

_____

DAY: MON TUES WED THU FRI SAT SUN

DATE

___/___/___

01 GRATITUDE
Today I am *Grateful* for:

_____

_____

02 MY ENERGY

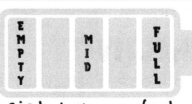

EMPTY   MID   FULL

My **Energy Level** today:

Circle how you feel

I feel this way because:

_____

_____

CIRCLE THE DAY

GRATTITUDE
with
Attitude

DAY: MON TUES WED THU FRI SAT SUN

DATE
_/_/_

01 GRATITUDE
Today I am *Grateful* for:

_____

_____

02 THANKFULNESS
This person helped me out today:

03 KNOWLEDGE & LEARNING
Today I learned:

_____

DAY: MON TUES WED THU FRI SAT SUN

DATE
_/_/_

01 GRATITUDE
Today I am *Grateful* for:

_____

02 CONNECTIVITY
How 'connected' did you feel to others today?

Tick a circle →

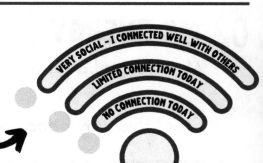

VERY SOCIAL – I CONNECTED WELL WITH OTHERS

LIMITED CONNECTION TODAY

NO CONNECTION TODAY

GRATTITUDE
with
Attitude

DAY: MON TUES WED THU FRI SAT SUN

DATE
___/___/___

01 GRATITUDE

Today I am *Grateful* for:

_____

_____

02 THANKFULNESS

This person helped me out today:

03 KNOWLEDGE & LEARNING

Today I learned:

_____

DAY: MON TUES WED THU FRI SAT SUN

DATE
___/___/___

01 GRATITUDE

Today I am *Grateful* for:

_____

_____

02 ACT OF KINDNESS

I helped this person out today:_____

I helped them by...

_____

GRATTITUDE
with
Attitude

CIRCLE THE DAY

DAY: MON TUES WED THU FRI SAT SUN

DATE ___ / ___ / ___

01 GRATITUDE
Today I am *Grateful* for:

_____

_____

02 THANKFULNESS
This person helped me out today:

03 KNOWLEDGE & LEARNING
Today I learned:

_____

DAY: MON TUES WED THU FRI SAT SUN

DATE ___ / ___ / ___

01 GRATITUDE
Today I am *Grateful* for:

_____

_____

02 THIS PUT A SMILE ON MY FACE
Today I smiled when:

_____

_____

GRATTITUDE
with
Attitude

DAY: MON TUES WED THU FRI SAT SUN

DATE
__ / __ / __

01 GRATITUDE
Today I am *Grateful* for:

_____

_____

02 THANKFULNESS
This person helped me out today:

03 KNOWLEDGE & LEARNING
Today I learned:

_____

DAY: MON TUES WED THU FRI SAT SUN

DATE
__ / __ / __

01 GRATITUDE
Today I am *Grateful* for:

_____

02 THIS PUT A SMILE ON MY FACE
Today I smiled when:

_____

_____

GRATTITUDE
with
Attitude

DAY: **MON TUES WED THU FRI SAT SUN**

DATE

___/___/___

01 GRATITUDE

Today I am *Grateful* for:

_____

_____

02 THANKFULNESS

This person helped me out today:

03 KNOWLEDGE & LEARNING

Today I learned:

_____

DAY: **MON TUES WED THU FRI SAT SUN**

DATE

___/___/___

01 GRATITUDE

Today I am *Grateful* for:

_____

_____

02 MY ENERGY

My **Energy Level** today:

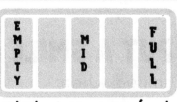

Circle how you feel

I feel this way because:

_____

_____

GRATTITUDE
with
Attitude

DAY: MON TUES WED THU FRI SAT SUN

DATE

___ / ___ / ___

01 GRATITUDE

Today I am *Grateful* for:

_____

_____

02 THANKFULNESS

This person helped me out today:

03 KNOWLEDGE & LEARNING

Today I learned:

_____

DAY: MON TUES WED THU FRI SAT SUN

DATE

___ / ___ / ___

01 GRATITUDE

Today I am *Grateful* for:

_____

_____

02 CONNECTIVITY

How 'connected' did you feel to others today?

Tick a circle →

VERY SOCIAL – I CONNECTED WELL WITH OTHERS

LIMITED CONNECTION TODAY

NO CONNECTION TODAY

GRATITUDE
with
Attitude

CIRCLE THE DAY

DAY: **MON TUES WED THU FRI SAT SUN**

DATE
___ / ___ / ___

01 GRATITUDE
Today I am *Grateful* for:

_____

_____

02 THANKFULNESS

This person helped me out today:

03 KNOWLEDGE & LEARNING
Today I learned:

_____

DAY: **MON TUES WED THU FRI SAT SUN**

DATE
___ / ___ / ___

01 GRATITUDE
Today I am *Grateful* for:

_____

_____

02 ACT OF KINDNESS
I helped this person out today:_____

I helped them by...

_____

DAY: MON TUES WED THU FRI SAT SUN

DATE
___/___/___

01 GRATITUDE
Today I am *Grateful* for:

_____

_____

02 THANKFULNESS
This person helped me out today:

03 KNOWLEDGE & LEARNING
Today I learned:

_____

DAY: MON TUES WED THU FRI SAT SUN

DATE
___/___/___

01 GRATITUDE
Today I am *Grateful* for:

_____

_____

02 THIS PUT A SMILE ON MY FACE
Today I smiled when:

_____

_____

GRATTITUDE
with
Attitude

DAY: MON TUES WED THU FRI SAT SUN

01 GRATITUDE
Today I am *Grateful* for:

_____

_____

02 THANKFULNESS
This person helped me out today:

03 KNOWLEDGE & LEARNING
Today I learned:

_____

DAY: MON TUES WED THU FRI SAT SUN

01 GRATITUDE
Today I am *Grateful* for:

_____

02 THIS PUT A SMILE ON MY FACE
Today I smiled when:

_____

_____

 **CIRCLE THE DAY**

GRATTITUDE
with
Attitude

DAY: MON TUES WED THU FRI SAT SUN

01 GRATITUDE

Today I am *Grateful* for:

DATE

___ / ___ / ___

_____

_____

02 THANKFULNESS

This person helped me out today:

03 KNOWLEDGE & LEARNING

Today I learned:

_____

DAY: MON TUES WED THU FRI SAT SUN

01 GRATITUDE

Today I am *Grateful* for:

DATE

___ / ___ / ___

_____

_____

02 MY ENERGY

My **Energy Level** today:

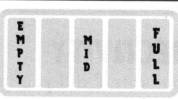

Circle how you feel

I feel this way because:

_____

_____

CIRCLE THE DAY

GRATTITUDE with Attitude

DAY: MON TUES WED THU FRI SAT SUN

01 GRATITUDE

Today I am *Grateful* for:

DATE

___/___/___

_____

_____

02 THANKFULNESS

This person helped me out today:

03 KNOWLEDGE & LEARNING

Today I learned:

_____

DAY: MON TUES WED THU FRI SAT SUN

DATE

01 GRATITUDE

Today I am *Grateful* for:

___/___/___

_____

_____

02 CONNECTIVITY

How 'connected' did you feel to others today?

Tick a circle ➤

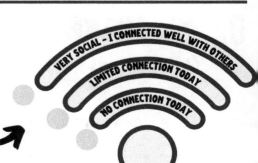

VERY SOCIAL – I CONNECTED WELL WITH OTHERS

LIMITED CONNECTION TODAY

NO CONNECTION TODAY

GRATTITUDE
with
Attitude

DAY: MON TUES WED THU FRI SAT SUN

DATE
/ /

01 GRATITUDE
Today I am *Grateful* for:

_____

_____

02 THANKFULNESS
This person helped me out today:

03 KNOWLEDGE & LEARNING
Today I learned:

_____

DAY: MON TUES WED THU FRI SAT SUN

DATE
/ /

01 GRATITUDE
Today I am *Grateful* for:

_____

_____

02 ACT OF KINDNESS
I helped this person out today: _____

I helped them by...

_____

GRATTITUDE
with
Attitude

DAY: MON TUES WED THU FRI SAT SUN

DATE
___/___/___

01 GRATITUDE
Today I am *Grateful* for:

_____

_____

02 THANKFULNESS
This person helped me out today:

03 KNOWLEDGE & LEARNING
Today I learned:

_____

DAY: MON TUES WED THU FRI SAT SUN

DATE
___/___/___

01 GRATITUDE
Today I am *Grateful* for:

_____

02 THIS PUT A SMILE ON MY FACE
Today I smiled when:

_____

_____

GRATTITUDE
with
Attitude

DAY: MON TUES WED THU FRI SAT SUN

01 GRATITUDE

Today I am *Grateful* for:

DATE

___/___/___

_____

_____

02 THANKFULNESS

This person helped me out today:

03 KNOWLEDGE & LEARNING

Today I learned:

_____

DAY: MON TUES WED THU FRI SAT SUN

01 GRATITUDE

Today I am *Grateful* for:

DATE

___/___/___

_____

_____

02 THIS PUT A SMILE ON MY FACE

Today I smiled when:

_____

_____

GRATTITUDE
with
Attitude

DAY: MON TUES WED THU FRI SAT SUN

DATE

___/___/___

01 GRATITUDE

Today I am *Grateful* for:

_____

_____

02 THANKFULNESS

This person helped me out today:

03 KNOWLEDGE & LEARNING

Today I learned:

_____

DAY: MON TUES WED THU FRI SAT SUN

DATE

___/___/___

01 GRATITUDE

Today I am *Grateful* for:

_____

_____

02 MY ENERGY

My **Energy Level** today:

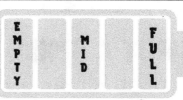

Circle how you feel

I feel this way because:

_____

_____

 **CIRCLE THE DAY**

GRATTITUDE
with
Attitude

DAY: MON TUES WED THU FRI SAT SUN

 **DATE**

/ /

01 GRATITUDE
Today I am *Grateful* for:

_____

_____

02 THANKFULNESS
This person helped me out today:

03 KNOWLEDGE & LEARNING
Today I learned:

_____

DAY: MON TUES WED THU FRI SAT SUN

DATE

/ /

01 GRATITUDE
Today I am *Grateful* for:

_____

_____

02 CONNECTIVITY
How 'connected' did you feel to others today?

VERY SOCIAL – I CONNECTED WELL WITH OTHERS

LIMITED CONNECTION TODAY

NO CONNECTION TODAY

Tick a circle

DAY: MON TUES WED THU FRI SAT SUN

01 GRATITUDE

Today I am *Grateful* for:

DATE

___ / ___ / ___

_____

_____

02 THANKFULNESS

This person helped me out today:

03 KNOWLEDGE & LEARNING

Today I learned:

_____

DAY: MON TUES WED THU FRI SAT SUN

01 GRATITUDE

Today I am *Grateful* for:

DATE

___ / ___ / ___

_____

_____

02 ACT OF KINDNESS

I helped this person out today: _____

I helped them by...

_____

GRATTITUDE with Attitude

CIRCLE THE DAY

DAY: MON TUES WED THU FRI SAT SUN

DATE ___/___/___

01 GRATITUDE
Today I am *Grateful* for:

_____

_____

02 THANKFULNESS
This person helped me out today:

03 KNOWLEDGE & LEARNING
Today I learned:

_____

DAY: MON TUES WED THU FRI SAT SUN

DATE ___/___/___

01 GRATITUDE
Today I am *Grateful* for:

_____

02 THIS PUT A SMILE ON MY FACE
Today I smiled when:

_____

_____

GRATTITUDE
with
Attitude

CIRCLE THE DAY

DAY: MON TUES WED THU FRI SAT SUN

DATE
___/___/___

01 GRATITUDE
Today I am *Grateful* for:

_____

_____

02 THANKFULNESS
This person helped me out today:

03 KNOWLEDGE & LEARNING
Today I learned:

_____

DAY: MON TUES WED THU FRI SAT SUN

DATE
___/___/___

01 GRATITUDE
Today I am *Grateful* for:

_____

_____

02 THIS PUT A SMILE ON MY FACE
Today I smiled when:

_____

_____

GRATTITUDE
with
Attitude

DAY: MON TUES WED THU FRI SAT SUN

DATE

/ /

01 GRATITUDE

Today I am *Grateful* for:

_____

_____

02 THANKFULNESS

This person helped me out today:

03 KNOWLEDGE & LEARNING

Today I learned:

_____

DAY: MON TUES WED THU FRI SAT SUN

DATE

/ /

01 GRATITUDE

Today I am *Grateful* for:

_____

_____

02 MY ENERGY

My **Energy Level** today:

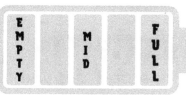

Circle how you feel

I feel this way because:

_____

_____

GRATTITUDE
with
Attitude

DAY: MON TUES WED THU FRI SAT SUN

DATE

___ / ___ / ___

01 GRATITUDE

Today I am *Grateful* for:

_____

_____

02 THANKFULNESS

This person helped me out today:

03 KNOWLEDGE & LEARNING

Today I learned:

_____

DAY: MON TUES WED THU FRI SAT SUN

DATE

___ / ___ / ___

01 GRATITUDE

Today I am *Grateful* for:

_____

_____

02 CONNECTIVITY

How 'connected' did you feel to others today?

Tick a circle ➜

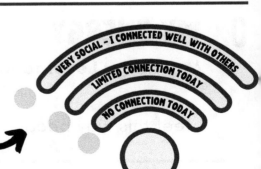

VERY SOCIAL - I CONNECTED WELL WITH OTHERS

LIMITED CONNECTION TODAY

NO CONNECTION TODAY

GRATTITUDE
with
Attitude

DAY: MON TUES WED THU FRI SAT SUN

DATE __ / __ / __

01 GRATITUDE
Today I am *Grateful* for:

_____

_____

02 THANKFULNESS
This person helped me out today:

03 KNOWLEDGE & LEARNING
Today I learned:

_____

DAY: MON TUES WED THU FRI SAT SUN

DATE __ / __ / __

01 GRATITUDE
Today I am *Grateful* for:

_____

_____

02 ACT OF KINDNESS
I helped this person out today: _____

I helped them by...

_____

GRATTITUDE with Attitude

CIRCLE THE DAY

DAY: MON TUES WED THU FRI SAT SUN

DATE ___ / ___ / ___

01 GRATITUDE
Today I am *Grateful* for:

_____

_____

02 THANKFULNESS
This person helped me out today:

03 KNOWLEDGE & LEARNING
Today I learned:

_____

DAY: MON TUES WED THU FRI SAT SUN

DATE ___ / ___ / ___

01 GRATITUDE
Today I am *Grateful* for:

_____

_____

02 THIS PUT A SMILE ON MY FACE
Today I smiled when:

_____

_____

GRATTITUDE
with
Attitude

DAY: MON TUES WED THU FRI SAT SUN

DATE
___/___/___

01 GRATITUDE
Today I am *Grateful* for:

_____

_____

02 THANKFULNESS
This person helped me out today:

03 KNOWLEDGE & LEARNING
Today I learned:

_____

DAY: MON TUES WED THU FRI SAT SUN

DATE
___/___/___

01 GRATITUDE
Today I am *Grateful* for:

_____

_____

02 THIS PUT A SMILE ON MY FACE
Today I smiled when:

_____

_____

CIRCLE THE DAY

GRATITUDE
with
Attitude

DAY: **MON TUES WED THU FRI SAT SUN**

DATE
___/___/___

01 GRATITUDE
Today I am *Grateful* for:

_____

_____

02 THANKFULNESS
This person helped me out today:

03 KNOWLEDGE & LEARNING
Today I learned:

_____

DAY: **MON TUES WED THU FRI SAT SUN**

DATE
___/___/___

01 GRATITUDE
Today I am *Grateful* for:

_____

_____

02 MY ENERGY
My **Energy Level** today:

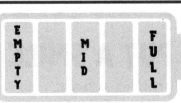

Circle how you feel

I feel this way because:

_____

_____

DAY: MON TUES WED THU FRI SAT SUN

01 GRATITUDE

DATE

___ / ___ / ___

Today I am *Grateful* for:

_____

_____

02 THANKFULNESS

This person helped me out today:

03 KNOWLEDGE & LEARNING

Today I learned:

_____

DAY: MON TUES WED THU FRI SAT SUN

DATE

___ / ___ / ___

01 GRATITUDE

Today I am *Grateful* for:

_____

_____

02 CONNECTIVITY

How 'connected' did you feel to others today?

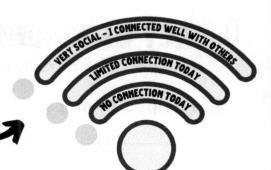

VERY SOCIAL - I CONNECTED WELL WITH OTHERS

LIMITED CONNECTION TODAY

NO CONNECTION TODAY

Tick a circle

GRATTITUDE
with
Attitude

CIRCLE THE DAY

DAY: MON TUES WED THU FRI SAT SUN

DATE / /

01 GRATITUDE
Today I am *Grateful* for:

_____

_____

02 THANKFULNESS
This person helped me out today:

03 KNOWLEDGE & LEARNING
Today I learned:

_____

DAY: MON TUES WED THU FRI SAT SUN

DATE / /

01 GRATITUDE
Today I am *Grateful* for:

_____

_____

02 ACT OF KINDNESS
I helped this person out today:_____

I helped them by...

_____

DAY: MON TUES WED THU FRI SAT SUN

DATE
___ / ___ / ___

01 GRATITUDE
Today I am *Grateful* for:

_____

_____

02 THANKFULNESS
This person helped me out today:

03 KNOWLEDGE & LEARNING
Today I learned:

_____

DAY: MON TUES WED THU FRI SAT SUN

DATE
___ / ___ / ___

01 GRATITUDE
Today I am *Grateful* for:

_____

_____

02 THIS PUT A SMILE ON MY FACE

Today I smiled when:

_____

_____

 **CIRCLE THE DAY**

GRATTITUDE
with
Attitude

DAY: MON TUES WED THU FRI SAT SUN

DATE
_____ / _____ / _____

01 GRATITUDE

Today I am *Grateful* for:

_____

_____

02 THANKFULNESS

This person helped me out today:

03 KNOWLEDGE & LEARNING

Today I learned:

_____

DAY: MON TUES WED THU FRI SAT SUN

DATE
_____ / _____ / _____

01 GRATITUDE

Today I am *Grateful* for:

_____

_____

02 THIS PUT A SMILE ON MY FACE

Today I smiled when:

_____

_____

GRATTITUDE
with
Attitude

DAY: MON TUES WED THU FRI SAT SUN

DATE

_____ / _____ / _____

01 GRATITUDE

Today I am *Grateful* for:

_____

_____

02 THANKFULNESS

This person helped me out today:

03 KNOWLEDGE & LEARNING

Today I learned:

_____

DAY: MON TUES WED THU FRI SAT SUN

DATE

_____ / _____ / _____

01 GRATITUDE

Today I am *Grateful* for:

_____

_____

02 MY ENERGY

My **Energy Level** today:

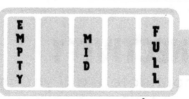

Circle how you feel

I feel this way because:

_____

_____

GRATTITUDE
with
Attitude

DAY: MON TUES WED THU FRI SAT SUN

DATE

/ /

01 GRATITUDE

Today I am *Grateful* for:

_____

_____

02 THANKFULNESS

This person helped me out today:

03 KNOWLEDGE & LEARNING

Today I learned:

_____

_____

DAY: MON TUES WED THU FRI SAT SUN

DATE

/ /

01 GRATITUDE

Today I am *Grateful* for:

_____

_____

02 CONNECTIVITY

How 'connected' did you feel to others today?

Tick a circle

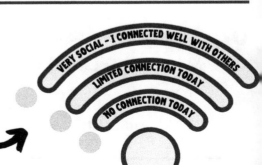

VERY SOCIAL - I CONNECTED WELL WITH OTHERS

LIMITED CONNECTION TODAY

NO CONNECTION TODAY

GRATTITUDE
with
Attitude

DAY: MON TUES WED THU FRI SAT SUN

01 GRATITUDE

Today I am *Grateful* for:

DATE

___ / ___ / ___

_____

_____

02 THANKFULNESS

This person helped me out today:

03 KNOWLEDGE & LEARNING

Today I learned:

_____

DAY: MON TUES WED THU FRI SAT SUN

01 GRATITUDE

Today I am *Grateful* for:

DATE

___ / ___ / ___

_____

_____

02 ACT OF KINDNESS

I helped this person out today: _____

I helped them by...

_____

DAY: MON TUES WED THU FRI SAT SUN

DATE

___/___/___

01 GRATITUDE
Today I am *Grateful* for:

_____

_____

02 THANKFULNESS
This person helped me out today:

03 KNOWLEDGE & LEARNING
Today I learned:

_____

DAY: MON TUES WED THU FRI SAT SUN

DATE

___/___/___

01 GRATITUDE
Today I am *Grateful* for:

_____

_____

02 THIS PUT A SMILE ON MY FACE

Today I smiled when:

_____

_____

GRATTITUDE
with
Attitude

DAY: MON TUES WED THU FRI SAT SUN

DATE

/ /

01 GRATITUDE
Today I am *Grateful* for:

_____

_____

02 THANKFULNESS
This person helped me out today:

03 KNOWLEDGE & LEARNING
Today I learned:

_____

DAY: MON TUES WED THU FRI SAT SUN

DATE

/ /

01 GRATITUDE
Today I am *Grateful* for:

_____

_____

02 THIS PUT A SMILE ON MY FACE
Today I smiled when:

_____

_____

GRATTITUDE
with
Attitude

DAY: MON TUES WED THU FRI SAT SUN

01 GRATITUDE

Today I am *Grateful* for:

DATE
___ / ___ / ___

_____

_____

02 THANKFULNESS

This person helped me out today:

03 KNOWLEDGE & LEARNING

Today I learned:

_____

DAY: MON TUES WED THU FRI SAT SUN

01 GRATITUDE

Today I am *Grateful* for:

DATE
___ / ___ / ___

_____

_____

02 MY ENERGY

My **Energy Level** today:

Circle how you feel

I feel this way because:

_____

GRATTITUDE
with
Attitude

CIRCLE THE DAY

DAY: MON TUES WED THU FRI SAT SUN

DATE
__/__/__

01 GRATITUDE
Today I am *Grateful* for:

_____

_____

02 THANKFULNESS
This person helped me out today:

03 KNOWLEDGE & LEARNING
Today I learned:

_____

DAY: MON TUES WED THU FRI SAT SUN

DATE
__/__/__

01 GRATITUDE
Today I am *Grateful* for:

_____

_____

02 CONNECTIVITY
How 'connected' did you feel to others today?

Tick a circle

VERY SOCIAL – I CONNECTED WELL WITH OTHERS
LIMITED CONNECTION TODAY
NO CONNECTION TODAY

GRATTITUDE
with
Attitude

DAY: MON TUES WED THU FRI SAT SUN

DATE
/ /

01 GRATITUDE

Today I am *Grateful* for:

_____

_____

02 THANKFULNESS

This person helped me out today:

03 KNOWLEDGE & LEARNING

Today I learned:

_____

DAY: MON TUES WED THU FRI SAT SUN

DATE
/ /

01 GRATITUDE

Today I am *Grateful* for:

_____

_____

02 ACT OF KINDNESS

I helped this person out today: _____

I helped them by...

_____

GRATTITUDE with Attitude

DAY: MON TUES WED THU FRI SAT SUN

DATE ___/___/___

01 GRATITUDE

Today I am *Grateful* for:

_____

_____

02 THANKFULNESS

This person helped me out today:

03 KNOWLEDGE & LEARNING

Today I learned:

_____

DAY: MON TUES WED THU FRI SAT SUN

DATE ___/___/___

01 GRATITUDE

Today I am *Grateful* for:

_____

_____

02 THIS PUT A SMILE ON MY FACE

Today I smiled when:

_____

_____

GRATTITUDE
with
Attitude

CIRCLE THE DAY

DAY: MON TUES WED THU FRI SAT SUN

DATE
___/___/___

01 GRATITUDE
Today I am *Grateful* for:

_____

_____

02 THANKFULNESS
This person helped me out today:

03 KNOWLEDGE & LEARNING
Today I learned:

_____

DAY: MON TUES WED THU FRI SAT SUN

DATE
___/___/___

01 GRATITUDE
Today I am *Grateful* for:

_____

_____

02 THIS PUT A SMILE ON MY FACE
Today I smiled when:

_____

_____

GRATTITUDE
with
Attitude

DAY: MON TUES WED THU FRI SAT SUN

DATE
___ / ___ / ___

01 GRATITUDE

Today I am *Grateful* for:

_____

_____

02 THANKFULNESS

This person helped me out today:

03 KNOWLEDGE & LEARNING

Today I learned:

_____

DAY: MON TUES WED THU FRI SAT SUN

DATE
___ / ___ / ___

01 GRATITUDE

Today I am *Grateful* for:

_____

_____

02 MY ENERGY

My **Energy Level** today:

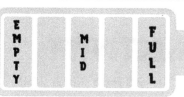

Circle how you feel

I feel this way because:

_____

_____

GRATTITUDE
with
Attitude

DAY: MON TUES WED THU FRI SAT SUN

DATE
___ / ___ / ___

01 GRATITUDE
Today I am *Grateful* for:

_____

_____

02 THANKFULNESS
This person helped me out today:

03 KNOWLEDGE & LEARNING
Today I learned:

_____

DAY: MON TUES WED THU FRI SAT SUN

DATE
___ / ___ / ___

01 GRATITUDE
Today I am *Grateful* for:

_____

_____

02 CONNECTIVITY
How 'connected' did you feel to others today?

Tick a circle ➜

VERY SOCIAL - I CONNECTED WELL WITH OTHERS

LIMITED CONNECTION TODAY

NO CONNECTION TODAY

GRATTITUDE
with
Attitude

DAY: MON TUES WED THU FRI SAT SUN

01 GRATITUDE

Today I am *Grateful* for:

DATE

___/___/___

_____

_____

02 THANKFULNESS

This person helped me out today:

03 KNOWLEDGE & LEARNING

Today I learned:

_____

DAY: MON TUES WED THU FRI SAT SUN

01 GRATITUDE

Today I am *Grateful* for:

DATE

___/___/___

_____

_____

02 ACT OF KINDNESS

I helped this person out today:_____

I helped them by...

_____

GRATTITUDE
with
Attitude

DAY: MON TUES WED THU FRI SAT SUN

DATE
__/__/__

01 GRATITUDE
Today I am *Grateful* for:

_____

_____

02 THANKFULNESS
This person helped me out today:

03 KNOWLEDGE & LEARNING
Today I learned:

_____

DAY: MON TUES WED THU FRI SAT SUN

DATE
__/__/__

01 GRATITUDE
Today I am *Grateful* for:

_____

_____

02 THIS PUT A SMILE ON MY FACE
Today I smiled when:

_____

_____

GRATTITUDE
with
Attitude

CIRCLE THE DAY

DAY: **MON TUES WED THU FRI SAT SUN**

DATE
___/___/___

01 GRATITUDE

Today I am *Grateful* for:

_____

_____

02 THANKFULNESS

This person helped me out today:

03 KNOWLEDGE & LEARNING

Today I learned:

_____

DAY: **MON TUES WED THU FRI SAT SUN**

DATE
___/___/___

01 GRATITUDE

Today I am *Grateful* for:

_____

_____

02 THIS PUT A SMILE ON MY FACE

Today I smiled when:

_____

_____

GRATTITUDE
with
Attitude

DAY: MON TUES WED THU FRI SAT SUN

DATE

___ / ___ / ___

01 GRATITUDE
Today I am *Grateful* for:

_____

_____

02 THANKFULNESS
This person helped me out today:

03 KNOWLEDGE & LEARNING
Today I learned:

_____

DAY: MON TUES WED THU FRI SAT SUN

DATE

___ / ___ / ___

01 GRATITUDE
Today I am *Grateful* for:

_____

_____

02 MY ENERGY
My **Energy Level** today:

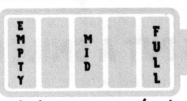

Circle how you feel

I feel this way because:

_____

_____

GRATTITUDE
with
Attitude

CIRCLE THE DAY

DAY: MON TUES WED THU FRI SAT SUN

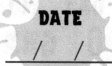

01 GRATITUDE

Today I am *Grateful* for:

DATE

___ / ___ / ___

_____

_____

02 THANKFULNESS

This person helped me out today:

03 KNOWLEDGE & LEARNING

Today I learned:

_____

DAY: MON TUES WED THU FRI SAT SUN

DATE

___ / ___ / ___

01 GRATITUDE

Today I am *Grateful* for:

_____

_____

02 CONNECTIVITY

How 'connected' did you feel to others today?

Tick a circle ➤

VERY SOCIAL – I CONNECTED WELL WITH OTHERS
LIMITED CONNECTION TODAY
NO CONNECTION TODAY

GRATTITUDE
with
Attitude

DAY: MON TUES WED THU FRI SAT SUN

DATE
/ /

01 GRATITUDE
Today I am *Grateful* for:

_____

_____

02 THANKFULNESS
This person helped me out today:

03 KNOWLEDGE & LEARNING
Today I learned:

_____

DAY: MON TUES WED THU FRI SAT SUN

DATE
/ /

01 GRATITUDE
Today I am *Grateful* for:

_____

_____

02 ACT OF KINDNESS
I helped this person out today: _____

I helped them by...

_____

GRATTITUDE
with
Attitude

CIRCLE THE DAY

DAY: MON TUES WED THU FRI SAT SUN

DATE
___/___/___

01 GRATITUDE
Today I am *Grateful* for:

_____

_____

02 THANKFULNESS
This person helped me out today:

03 KNOWLEDGE & LEARNING
Today I learned:

_____

DAY: MON TUES WED THU FRI SAT SUN

DATE
___/___/___

01 GRATITUDE
Today I am *Grateful* for:

_____

_____

02 THIS PUT A SMILE ON MY FACE
Today I smiled when:

_____

_____

GRATTITUDE
with
Attitude

DAY: **MON TUES WED THU FRI SAT SUN**

DATE
___/___/___

01 GRATITUDE
Today I am *Grateful* for:

_____

_____

02 THANKFULNESS
This person helped me out today:

03 KNOWLEDGE & LEARNING
Today I learned:

_____

DAY: **MON TUES WED THU FRI SAT SUN**

DATE
___/___/___

01 GRATITUDE
Today I am *Grateful* for:

_____

_____

02 THIS PUT A SMILE ON MY FACE
Today I smiled when:

_____

_____

GRATTITUDE
with
Attitude

DAY: MON TUES WED THU FRI SAT SUN

DATE
___ / ___ / ___

01 GRATITUDE
Today I am *Grateful* for:

_____

_____

02 THANKFULNESS
This person helped me out today:

03 KNOWLEDGE & LEARNING
Today I learned:

_____

DAY: MON TUES WED THU FRI SAT SUN

DATE
___ / ___ / ___

01 GRATITUDE
Today I am *Grateful* for:

_____

_____

02 MY ENERGY

My **Energy Level** today:

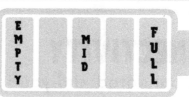

Circle how you feel

I feel this way because:

_____

_____

GRATTITUDE
with
Attitude

DAY: MON TUES WED THU FRI SAT SUN

DATE
/   /

01 GRATITUDE
Today I am *Grateful* for:

_____

_____

02 THANKFULNESS
This person helped me out today:

03 KNOWLEDGE & LEARNING
Today I learned:

_____

DAY: MON TUES WED THU FRI SAT SUN

DATE
/   /

01 GRATITUDE
Today I am *Grateful* for:

_____

_____

02 CONNECTIVITY
How 'connected' did you feel to others today?

Tick a circle

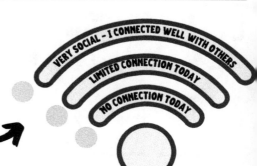

VERY SOCIAL - I CONNECTED WELL WITH OTHERS

LIMITED CONNECTION TODAY

NO CONNECTION TODAY

GRATTITUDE
with
Attitude

CIRCLE THE DAY

DAY: MON TUES WED THU FRI SAT SUN

DATE
___/___/___

01 GRATITUDE

Today I am *Grateful* for:

_____

_____

02 THANKFULNESS

This person helped me out today:

03 KNOWLEDGE & LEARNING

Today I learned:

_____

DAY: MON TUES WED THU FRI SAT SUN

DATE
___/___/___

01 GRATITUDE

Today I am *Grateful* for:

_____

_____

02 ACT OF KINDNESS

I helped this person out today: _____

I helped them by...

_____

GRATTITUDE
with Attitude

DAY: MON TUES WED THU FRI SAT SUN

DATE
/ /

01 GRATITUDE
Today I am *Grateful* for:

_____

_____

02 THANKFULNESS
This person helped me out today:

03 KNOWLEDGE & LEARNING
Today I learned:

_____

DAY: MON TUES WED THU FRI SAT SUN

DATE
/ /

01 GRATITUDE
Today I am *Grateful* for:

_____

_____

02 THIS PUT A SMILE ON MY FACE
Today I smiled when:

_____

_____

GRATTITUDE
with
Attitude

DAY: MON TUES WED THU FRI SAT SUN

DATE
___ / ___ / ___

01 GRATITUDE
Today I am *Grateful* for:

_____

_____

02 THANKFULNESS
This person helped me out today:

03 KNOWLEDGE & LEARNING
Today I learned:

_____

DAY: MON TUES WED THU FRI SAT SUN

DATE
___ / ___ / ___

01 GRATITUDE
Today I am *Grateful* for:

_____

_____

02 THIS PUT A SMILE ON MY FACE
Today I smiled when:

_____

_____

GRATTITUDE
with
Attitude

DAY: MON TUES WED THU FRI SAT SUN

DATE

___ / ___ / ___

01 GRATITUDE

Today I am *Grateful* for:

_____

_____

02 THANKFULNESS

This person helped me out today:

03 KNOWLEDGE & LEARNING

Today I learned:

_____

DAY: MON TUES WED THU FRI SAT SUN

DATE

___ / ___ / ___

01 GRATITUDE

Today I am *Grateful* for:

_____

_____

02 MY ENERGY

My **Energy Level** today:

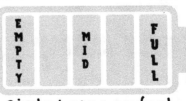

Circle how you feel

I feel this way because:

_____

_____

GRATTITUDE with Attitude

DAY: MON TUES WED THU FRI SAT SUN

DATE
___/___/___

01 GRATITUDE

Today I am *Grateful* for:

_____

_____

02 THANKFULNESS

This person helped me out today:

03 KNOWLEDGE & LEARNING

Today I learned:

_____

DAY: MON TUES WED THU FRI SAT SUN

DATE
___/___/___

01 GRATITUDE

Today I am *Grateful* for:

_____

_____

02 CONNECTIVITY

How 'connected' did you feel to others today?

Tick a circle →

VERY SOCIAL - I CONNECTED WELL WITH OTHERS
LIMITED CONNECTION TODAY
NO CONNECTION TODAY

GRATTITUDE
with
Attitude

DAY: MON TUES WED THU FRI SAT SUN

DATE

_____ / _____ / _____

01 GRATITUDE

Today I am *Grateful* for:

_____

_____

02 THANKFULNESS

This person helped me out today:

03 KNOWLEDGE & LEARNING

Today I learned:

_____

DAY: MON TUES WED THU FRI SAT SUN

DATE

_____ / _____ / _____

01 GRATITUDE

Today I am *Grateful* for:

_____

_____

02 ACT OF KINDNESS

I helped this person out today: _____

I helped them by...

_____

GRATTITUDE
with
Attitude

CIRCLE THE DAY

DAY: MON TUES WED THU FRI SAT SUN

DATE

/ /

01 GRATITUDE
Today I am *Grateful* for:

_____

_____

02 THANKFULNESS
This person helped me out today:

03 KNOWLEDGE & LEARNING
Today I learned:

_____

DAY: MON TUES WED THU FRI SAT SUN

DATE

/ /

01 GRATITUDE
Today I am *Grateful* for:

_____

_____

02 THIS PUT A SMILE ON MY FACE

Today I smiled when:

_____

_____

DAY: MON TUES WED THU FRI SAT SUN

DATE
___/___/___

01 GRATITUDE
Today I am *Grateful* for:

_____

_____

02 THANKFULNESS
This person helped me out today:

03 KNOWLEDGE & LEARNING
Today I learned:

_____

DAY: MON TUES WED THU FRI SAT SUN

DATE
___/___/___

01 GRATITUDE
Today I am *Grateful* for:

_____

02 THIS PUT A SMILE ON MY FACE
Today I smiled when:

_____

_____

200

WELL DONE! YOU HAVE COMPLETED 200 ENTRIES OF YOUR GRATITUDE JOURNAL. CONGRATULATIONS!!

It's time for you to reflect back over your past 200 gratitude entries.

MOMENTS/REFLECTIONS

What have been your highights?

01

_____

_____

_____

02

_____

_____

_____

03

_____

_____

_____

ACTIVITY

Write a short letter to someone that has been kind to you or someone you are grateful to have in your life. It may also be a photo you have, print up and write on the back?

This person will really appreciate that you have taken the time to show how much you appreciate them.

200 ENGRIES

Write some final notes on the next page. It's always great to reflect back on how you were feeling, the achievements you have made and what you have been grateful for over since starting your journal.

GRATITUDE WITH ATTITUDE

Journal Notes

Write here whatever you feel like. Is there something special you would like to include in your journal?

_____

_____

_____

_____

_____

_____

_____

"Nothing new can come into
your life unless you are
grateful for what you
already have"
- Michael Bernard

200 ENERIES

Write some final notes on the next page. It's always great to reflect back on how you were feeling, the achievements you have made and what you have been grateful for over since starting your journal.

GRATITUDE WITH ATTITUDE

Journal Notes

Write here whatever you feel like. Is there something special you would like to include in your journal?

_____

_____

_____

_____

_____

_____

_____

"Nothing new can come into
your life unless you are
grateful for what you
already have"
- Michael Bernard

GRATITUDE WITH ATTITUDE

Journal Notes

GRATITUDE WITH ATTITUDE

Journal Notes

About the Author

Romney Nelson is a #1 Amazon Best Selling Author and Leading Australian Goal Setting and Habit Development Expert. He commenced his career as a primary and secondary school teacher working in some of the most well-known schools in Australia, including Head of Faculty positions in Oxford and Wimbledon, United Kingdom.

Romney authored his first resource, PE on the GO; a physical education resource for teachers in 2009 and in 2019 in founded The Life Graduate Publishing Group and created The Daily Goal Tracker, a powerful and practical resource developed to Create, Track and Achieve your goals. In 2020, Romney became an Amazon Best Selling Author with the release of The Habit Switch. His other books include Magnetic Goals, The Daily Goal Tracker, The 5 Minute Morning Journal and various educational and children's books.

www.thelifegraduate.com/bookstore

Gratitude Journals by Romney Nelson

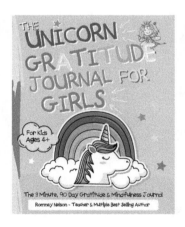